headwork reading non-fiction

A day in the life of an Undertaker

Chris Culshaw

OXFORD
UNIVERSITY PRESS

Headwork Reading Non-fiction

Series editor: Chris Culshaw

This series offers accessible and motivating texts based on real-life people and events.

It deliberately covers a range of non-fiction genres: correspondence, diaries and interviews, to act as models for students' reading and writing.

Titles in the series:

Dan Barlow	**A Greenpeace Logbook**
Chris Culshaw	**A Day in the Life of an Undertaker**
Rachel Duncan	**E-mails from Antarctica**
Kay Hill	**Postcards from India**
David Lord	**What Does a Bodyguard Really Do?**
Lisa Pote	**Diary of a Sponsored Bike Ride**

Author focus

Chris Culshaw

Chris is series editor for Headwork Reading, and wrote this text after interviewing a young undertaker working in a family firm.

The interview reveals what an undertaker really does day to day, and why it's such an important and satisfying job.

How on earth did you get into this work?

I started six years ago, when I was sixteen. My friends said things like: 'A funeral director? Isn't that a dead end job?' Some of them still think I must be mad, a bit of a weirdo even. But I like the work. No day is ever the same. It's a secure job too. I'll never be out of work. The first thing I had to learn is you don't become a funeral director overnight. It takes time. You need a lot of experience – behind the scenes. My boss always says, 'You need a few grey hairs to be a funeral director.'

What kind of things did you have to do when you first started?

At first all I did was clean the limos, polish the hearse, make tea. It was a bit boring. But lots of jobs are like that. 'You've got to walk before you can run.' That's what the boss said. So I had to do all the odd jobs. Office work. Answering the phone. There's a knack to that. People are often very upset when they ring. You have to know just what to say and how to say it. It's not like selling double glazing. Then the boss taught me how to line the coffins and fit coffin

handles. I like doing this because I'm good with my hands. Funeral directors used to make their own coffins. Now we buy them ready made, and finish them to suit the client's needs. They're a very traditional shape and usually quite plain. In Italy coffins have very ornate carvings. In the USA they use metal 'caskets'. I saw one in a catalogue. It cost $2000 and had a painting of *The Last Supper* inside the lid! Nowadays some people ask for cardboard coffins. These don't have handles and they can be very slippery in the rain. Very tricky to carry.

Do you lay out bodies?

Yes. After about six months I started to help the boss 'lay out'. I'd never seen a dead body before, so the first one was a bit of a shock. An old lady. Very small, almost like a doll, with bright red nail varnish. The boss said, 'Always remember this is a person, not a body.'

The bodies are brought to our chapel of rest. We start by washing the body. We use cool water and special soap to kill the bacteria. We clean the finger nails and wash the hair. The first time I did this I was

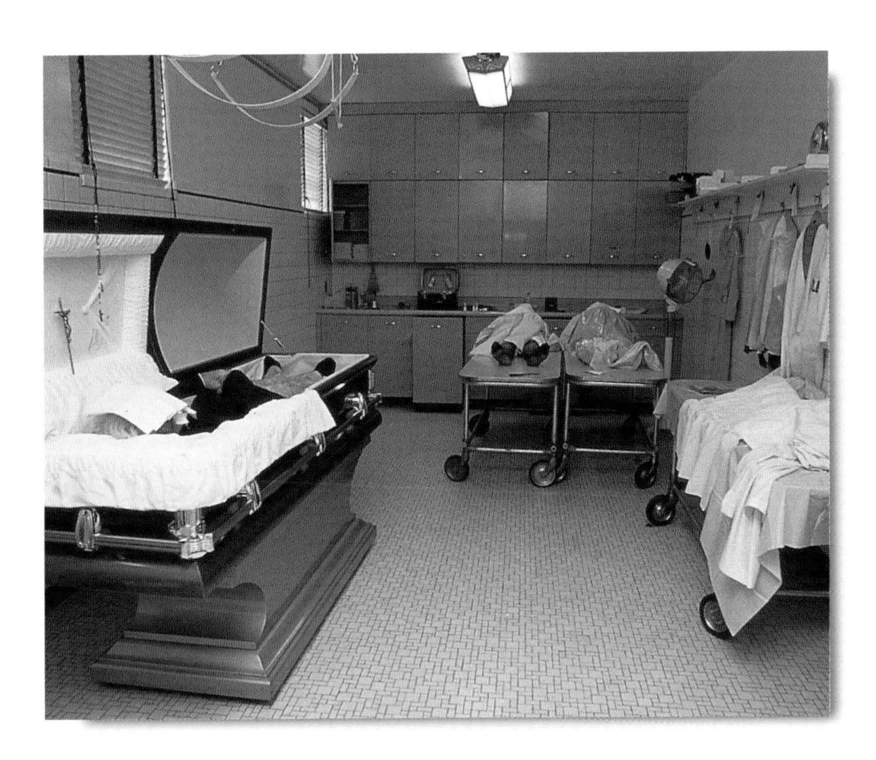

very nervous. It's such a personal thing. Most people think that dead bodies smell. They don't – not for three or four days at least. In very hot countries, where they don't have cold stores, they have to bury or cremate very quickly. We always handle the body very carefully. Everything has to be done in a dignified way. The boss has a good saying: 'Always behave as if the relatives are looking over your shoulder.'

The deceased arrive wearing a paper gown if they died in hospital. That always makes me sad. Very impersonal in a way. They might be wearing pyjamas, if they died at home. We dress them according to the relatives' wishes. We put on a full set of clothes: underwear, socks and shoes. Last week we buried an 'old soldier' in full dress uniform. Medals, cap and all. It was hard to get that just right. It can be a bit tricky to dress the body sometimes, because it goes stiff. We might have to cut the clothes, up the back, so the relatives don't see. Sometimes we are asked to dress the deceased in their Sunday best frock or suit. Other times it's jeans and t-shirt. One young chap was buried in a Manchester United strip. And the relatives put his football boots in the grave. A very nice touch, I thought.

We always comb the hair . This is very difficult to get just right and relatives always notice when it isn't.

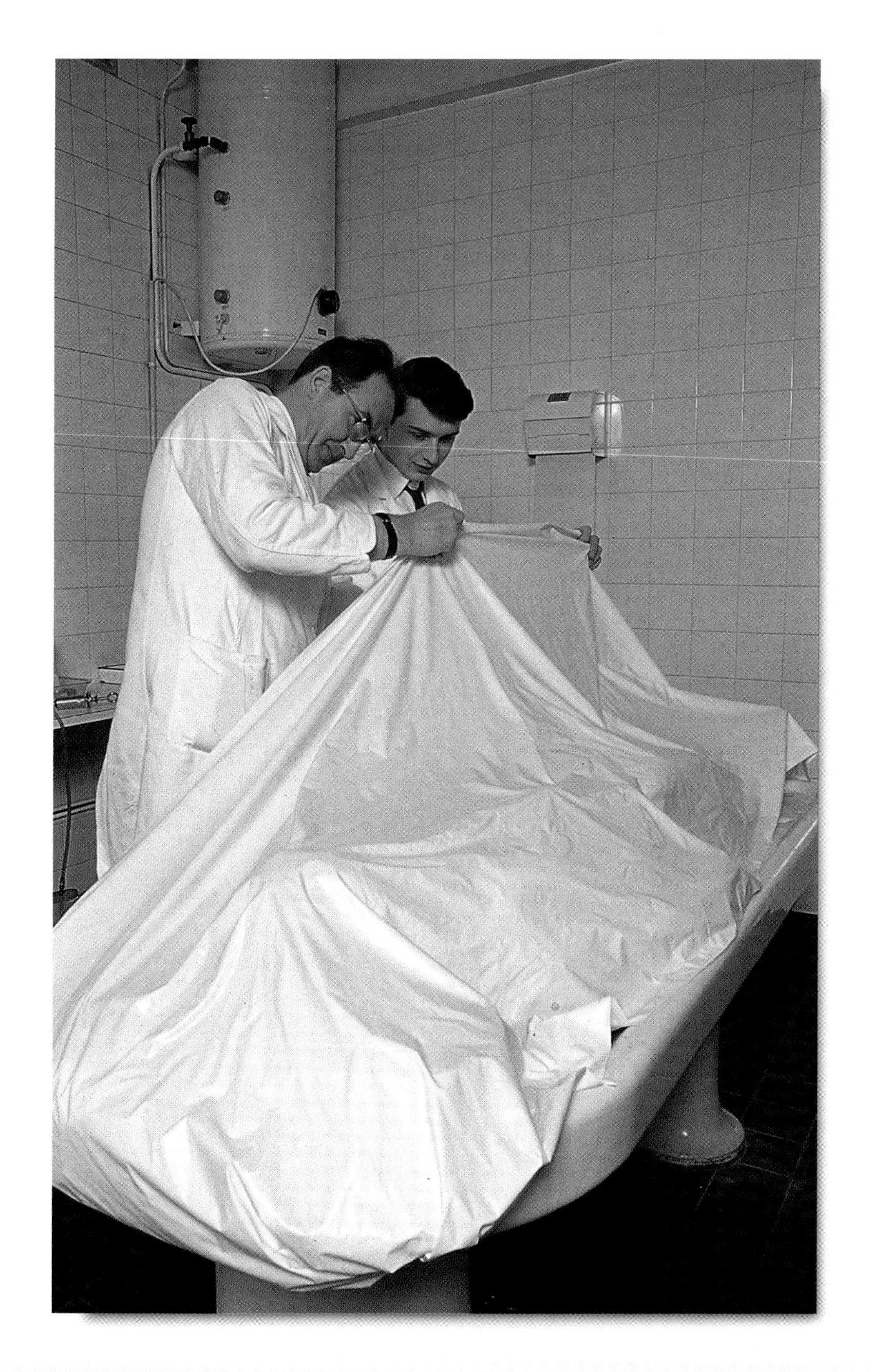

Death does change a face, especially after a long illness. We have to warn relatives about that. 'Illness does take its toll.' That's what the boss says. We use make-up – but not much. There's special make-up for funerals. We use ordinary face powder, from Boots. The trick is to soften the face without changing it. We try to place the hands so they look natural, as if the person's asleep.

Little details can be so important. Like remembering to put their false teeth in. A little girl once said to me, 'That's not my gran! My gran wears glasses. Even when she's got her eyes closed.' She was very upset. I won't make that mistake again.

Do you need to to be able to drive?

Yes. It's important. I got my licence when I was eighteen. The boss helped with the cost of lessons. He's kind like that. I'm old enough and experienced enough to drive the hearse now. That's a big responsibility. You've got to drive very carefully when there's a coffin on board. It would be awful for the family if you had a bump – even a small one. And the hearse costs over forty thousand pounds. So I'm always a bit nervous when I'm driving. No bad thing, I suppose. I'm not old enough to drive the limos yet. You have to have a special licence for that. It's also my job to make sure the right coffin gets put in the hearse. Every coffin has a metal disk with the name

engraved on it. If it's a cardboard coffin we write the name on it with a marker pen. Mistakes are made – very occasionally – and the wrong body ends up at the church.

Can you describe a typical week?

There's no such thing as 'a typical week' in this job. That why I like it. We have weeks when nobody dies. The boss cracks the same old joke: 'I think the phone must be out of order.' In an average week we organise three or four funerals. Each death means the boss has to make four or five visits to the family. He's often called out in the middle of the night. It's a 24-hours-a-day-job. It's years since he took a holiday. We tend to be busy during very cold weather, and also when it's very hot. I did five funerals in one day last year. That was a very long day! You may be tired or bored, but you can't show it. You are on show all the time. People expect you to be very smartly dressed. Short back and sides. Dark suit. Polished shoes. You've got to give 100%. The relatives would be very upset if everything wasn't just right.

Don't you ever get upset?

Of course. It's only natural. I wouldn't be human if I didn't get upset. You've got to be able to hide your feelings. You've got to be professional. I get very upset sometimes. I always think it's sad when someone dies and there's no family or friends at the funeral. When that happens we act as mourners and make sure everything is done right. Most of the funerals we do are old people. But burying a little child – that's something else. Cot deaths and the like. I'll never get used to them. It's like a hammer to the heart. Such tiny white coffins, some no bigger than a shoe box sometimes. We don't use a hearse for a child. We put the coffin on the back seat of the limo.

Can women become funeral directors?

Yes. Most funeral directors are men. Only about 5% are women. I know it sounds sexist to say 'it's a man's job' but it does involve a lot of heavy lifting. Last week we were called to a house where a 22-stone man had collapsed behind the bathroom door. We had to take the door off its hinges. It was very hard work getting him into the coffin. Then we had to get that coffin down two flights of steep, narrow stairs. And it all had to be done with dignity. The boss always says, 'Whatever happens – don't let go.'

When we get called to a house to remove a body we use an unmarked van. A dark blue Transit. We always wear surgical gloves. It's my job to stock the van with gloves. We wrap the body in a sheet and strap it on a special stretcher. If we can't get the stretcher into the house, then we use a plastic zip-up body bag.

We always ask the relatives if they want the coffin carried or wheeled at the funeral. Sometimes relatives want to carry the coffin. This isn't as easy as it looks. A body really is a 'dead weight'.

Do you embalm bodies?

The boss does. I don't. You need to go on a special training course to learn how to embalm. I'm hoping to go on one next year. Embalming is a real skill. It helps to preserve the appearance of the body. Most

bodies are not fully embalmed – just the head and hands. The parts the relatives see. You replace the blood in the body with a special pink fluid. This makes the body last longer.

Are most people cremated?

Yes. About three quarters of people are cremated. Relatives will often place teddy bears, letters, poems and photographs in the coffin. But we have to be very careful not to include anything which might explode, such as batteries in toys or watches. There are very strict rules about this. Somebody wanted to put a bottle of beer in their granddad's coffin. We had to say no. Pity. It was such a nice personal touch. But we've got to stick to the rules.

It takes over 2 hours to cremate a body. The furnace is very hot – 1800° F. There is nothing left of the coffin. The body is reduced to about 7 lbs of white chalky powder. Fillings, wedding rings and the like, all melt. You hear lots of horror stories about what goes on behind the scenes at a crematorium. A woman once said to me, 'Is it true they take the body out of the coffin before they burn it, so the undertaker can sell it again?' Of course we don't!

What is the hardest thing about the job?

The paperwork. There's a lot more to the job than I thought. There's a lot to learn. Lots of rules and regulations. Relatives will ask your advice about all sorts of things. A lady wanted to bury her husband in her back garden. This is very unusual, but it can be done. You have to have permission from the council and the water company. A body will last for over 75 years in the ground, so a plan of the grave must be added to the deeds of the house. There are rules about gravestones too. You can't make them out of wood or concrete. The wording on a headstone must

be respectful. After all, a cemetery is a special place. Nicknames are allowed. I saw one last week which said, 'Goodnight, Panhead. We all love you.'

'Woodland burials' are becoming quite popular now. There's no headstone for these. A tree is planted over the grave instead. I think this is very good idea. I'd rather have a row of trees than a row of gravestones.

Are you afraid of death?

It may seem a strange thing to say, but I never think about it. It's just part of the job. People react to death in different ways. We buried this young chap last

EMILY
1922.
WIFE.

year. His mother can't accept that he's dead. She still sets a place for him at the table every day. Keeps his room just as it was when he died. Some people get very angry. Angry with us. Angry with the doctors and nurses. Angry with everyone. Others try to keep busy. That helps.

Some seem relieved – happy, almost. Especially at the end of a long illness. It isn't always 'doom and gloom'. We once had a birthday party in the chapel of rest. An old man died a few days before his 80th. So the family came with their presents and a bottle of champagne. Some people might say that wasn't right or proper. I thought it was moving. It was what the family wanted, and that's what matters.

You never know how people will react. You've got to be prepared for anything. You need to be a bit of a diplomat too. Funerals can be very stressful for some families. I once pulled up outside a house in the limo and a woman came out in tears, crying, "I'm not going in the same car as her!" You just have to keep calm. 'Dignified – no matter what,' that's what the boss says. It's not always easy.

What's the most important skill you need?

Listening. You have to be a good listener to do this job. Most of our time is spent just listening. You've got to be confident. If someone is in shock because

their wife has died they want me to take charge. Organise things for them. So attention to detail is very important, and timing. A funeral involves a lot of very careful planning. Everything must go like clockwork. Most funerals take place less than a week after the death. There is a lot to be organised in that time.

The boss really loves his job. He gets a lot of satisfaction out of helping people. Everyone knows him round here. People see him as a friend. He's a rock. I think that's why I came into the job. I want to be like him. Respect – that's what it's all about.

How do you think your job will change in the future?

As I said, the most important part of the job is dealing with people. I don't think that will change. I don't think I'll ever be out of a job, do you? Not unless scientists find a way to make us live for ever! Some very rich people have their bodies frozen when they die. They think we'll find a 'cure' for death in the future, and they'll be brought back to life. Who knows what might happen?

Funerals will change though, and cemeteries. I saw an advert the other day for 'audio headstones'. You can have your last words recorded on a special tape, which is put into your gravestone. When friends and family visit the grave, they just press a button and

hear your voice. It sounds a bit weird to me, a bit spooky. But some people might like it.

There's a company in America that will scatter your ashes in outer space for you – if you're a dollar millionaire. And I suspect we'll have internet funerals before long, on the worldwide web. You'll be able to log on and pay your last respects. Not my cup of tea. I'm a bit old -fashioned when it comes to funerals!